This Book Belongs to

The mission of Storey Communications is to serve our customers
by publishing practical information that encourages personal independence
in harmony with the environment.

Edited by Pamela Lappies
Cover and interior illustrations by Mary Rich
Cover and text design by Meredith Maker
Text production by Susan Bernier
Indexed by Northwind Editorial Services

Some recipes have been adapted from other Storey/ Garden Way Publishing books: pages 6, 44: *The Pleasure of Herbs* by Phyllis V. Shaudys; page 16: *Satisfying Soups: Homemade Bisques, Chowders, Gumbos, Stews & More* by Phyllis Hobson; pages 18, 28, 32, 42: *The Joy of Gardening Cookbook* by Janet Ballantyne; pages 34, 58: *Tomatoes! 365 Healthy Recipes for Year-Round Enjoyment* by the Editors of Garden Way Publishing; page 48: *Weekend! A Menu Cookbook for Relaxed Entertaining* by Edith Stovel and Pamela Wakefield.

The information in this book is true and complete to the best of our knowledge. All recommendations are made without guarantee on the part of the author or Storey Communications, Inc. The author and publisher disclaim any liability in connection with the use of this information. For additional information please contact Storey Communications, Inc., Schoolhouse Road, Pownal, Vermont 05261.

Printed in Canada by Métropole Litho
10 9 8 7 6 5 4 3 2 1

**Library of Congress
Cataloging-in-Publication Data**

Bass, Ruth, 1934–
    Onions love herbs / Ruth Bass ;
    illustrations by Mary Rich.
              p.   cm.
    "A fresh from the garden cookbook."
    ISBN 0-88266-934-6 (hc : alk. paper)
    1. Cookery (Onions)   2. Cookery
    (Herbs)   I. Title.
TX803.O5B367 1996
641.6'525—dc20   96-14311
                                          CIP

ONIONS LOVE HERBS

A
Fresh from the Garden
Cookbook

RUTH BASS

ILLUSTRATED BY MARY RICH

STOREY

A Storey Publishing Book
Storey Communications, Inc.

Introduction

If the onion family held a reunion, it would be larger than when Winnie the Pooh's friend Rabbit brought together all his friends and relations. Add herbs, and it would take a stadium to hold everyone.

For centuries, the hundreds of species that belong to the allium family have had a place in medicinal remedies, garlic being hailed as the cure for almost anything — in addition to its value in warding off vampires. Herbalists say scallions are excellent for the digestion; onions, for protection against infection and to reduce blood pressure.

Whatever their value medicinally, onions, shallots, chives, scallions, leeks, and garlic are at home with most herbs in and out of the garden. And, indeed, since they're not much trouble and don't take up a lot of space, they ought to have a prominent place in the kitchen garden.

Chives, a perennial, work nicely in a flower or rock garden, with their round lavender flowers appearing early in the season. In the main garden, onions — Spanish, yellow, and red — can be grown from seed, plants, or sets. Garlic varies from one garden to the next, with some gardeners sold on planting in the fall for the next year's harvest. Shallots are prolific: Just poke a few from the kitchen supply into the ground, twelve inches apart.

Grown throughout the world, onions appear in the cookbooks and traditions of cuisines from China to the Middle East to South America. They crop up in soups, salads, and main dishes and do yeoman service either in the leading role or in a small part to add character. Cast them with cilantro, parsley, sage, or thyme, and they turn into stars — in an omelette, a soup, a stew, or a salad.

Here are some hints for getting along with the allium family in the kitchen:

1. Select onions individually so you won't get any soft ones. The area around the stem should be firm.

2. Avoid garlic that is shriveled. That means it's old and may be dried up under the papery skin and has less flavor. The same goes for shallots.

3. Leeks gather sand inside their many layers. Cutting them lengthwise and sluicing them with water is essential.

4. Try peeling onions under running water to avoid getting weepy. Or cut the end off a plastic bag, put the onion inside, and don the bag like a muff, peeling the onion inside it. Drop small onions or quantities of shallots into boiling water for a minute, remove, and rinse with cold water; the skins will slip off easily.

5. For garlic that will be chopped or minced, crush the clove with the flat of a knife and watch the skin slide off.

6. If you slice garlic open and find a green shoot starting in the center, take it out. It has a strong taste.

7. Don't chop onions in the food processor unless you want mush. You can do garlic and shallots that way, however.

Scallion Omelette with Marjoram

The oils remain in dried herbs, so they are more concentrated than fresh ones. If you can't find fresh marjoram for this omelette, use dried and cut the amount in half. Marjoram is a cousin to oregano but has a more delicate taste.

2 tablespoons extra virgin olive oil	2 teaspoons minced fresh marjoram
½ cup chopped scallions, green and white parts	8 eggs
	½ cup water
2 ripe tomatoes, chopped	Salt and freshly ground pepper
1 cup crumbled feta cheese	3 tablespoons butter

1. In a medium-size skillet, heat the oil and sauté the scallions and tomatoes for about 3 minutes, or until they are soft.
2. Remove from heat and stir in the feta cheese and marjoram. Set aside.
3. Beat the eggs until they are pale yellow. With a fork, blend in the water and salt and pepper to taste.
4. In a large skillet, melt the butter and, when it is foamy, pour in the egg mixture. Cook over medium heat until set, lifting the edges with a spatula to let the uncooked eggs run underneath. Spread the tomato and scallion mixture over the middle of the omelette and fold one half over the other.
5. Serve immediately on a preheated platter.

4 SERVINGS

Shallots and Tarragon Omelette

If there's a person in your house who can't eat eggs because of cholesterol concerns, do what the restaurants do: Use egg substitute. Though yellow in color, they're actually only the whites. Cook them with shallots and herbs, and the egg lover will no longer be deprived.

Vegetable spray
1 shallot, finely chopped
1 carton egg substitute
1 teaspoon minced fresh tarragon

1. Coat a medium-size skillet with the vegetable spray, heat, and add the chopped shallot. Cook slowly for about 10 minutes, less if you want the shallots to be crunchy.
2. Pour in the egg substitute and cook on low heat, lifting the edges to let the uncooked eggs run underneath. At the last minute, sprinkle the tarragon over the top and fold it in half like an omelette. Serve immediately.

2 SERVINGS

Turnovers and Thyme

Freshly baked turnovers enclosing a tasty filling are appealing little pockets. Choose a favorite mushroom, and for variety substitute chervil or savory for the thyme.

> ¼ cup low-fat cream cheese, at room temperature
> 2 sticks butter
> 1½ cups plus 2 tablespoons sifted unbleached all-purpose white flour
> 2 medium yellow onions, minced
> ½ pound fresh mushroom caps and stems, minced
> ½ teaspoon salt
> 1 teaspoon minced fresh thyme
> 2 teaspoons minced fresh parsley
> 1 garlic clove, minced
> ¼ cup yogurt
> 1 egg, beaten

1. In a food processor, combine the cream cheese, all but 3 tablespoons of the butter, and all but 2 tablespoons of the flour until a soft dough forms. Wrap in wax paper and refrigerate at least 1 hour.
2. Preheat the oven to 450°F.

3. In a saucepan, melt the remaining 3 tablespoons of butter and sauté the onions for 2 minutes. Add the mushrooms and cook until both are tender.
4. Stir in the salt, thyme, parsley, garlic, and the remaining 2 tablespoons of flour. Turn off the heat. Add the yogurt, stirring to combine.
5. On a lightly floured board, roll out half the dough to a ¼-inch thickness. Cut into 4-inch squares, and place a teaspoon of the mushroom mixture on each. Brush the edges with egg and fold the dough over, forming triangles.
6. Press the edges closed with the tines of a fork, making a border. Prick the tops with two or three small holes, and place them on an ungreased cookie sheet. Brush the tops with egg.
7. Continue this process with the rest of the dough, baking each batch as it is completed. Bake for 12 to 15 minutes, or until golden.

ABOUT 4 DOZEN

Cheesy Bread with Thyme

Here's a classy way to change an old-fashioned baking-powder biscuit into a cheesy bread flavored with poppy seeds and thyme. Poppy seeds are a commodity that can be traced all the way back to the Sumerians, who described their medicinal uses of the plant on clay tablets.

> 1   stick butter
> 1   large yellow onion, chopped (½ cup)
> 1   egg, lightly beaten
> ½   cup buttermilk
> 1½   cups unbleached all-purpose flour
> 2   teaspoons baking powder
> 4   ounces sharp cheddar cheese, shredded (1 cup)
> 3   tablespoons minced fresh thyme
> 1   tablespoon poppy seeds

1. Preheat the oven to 350°F, and grease an 8-inch square pan.
2. In a small skillet, melt 1 tablespoon of the butter and sauté the onion until it is soft and golden.
3. Combine the egg and buttermilk in a large bowl.
4. In a separate bowl, sift together the flour and baking powder, and cut in 5 tablespoons of the butter. Blend into the egg and buttermilk mixture.

5. Add the onion and ½ cup of the cheese.
6. Melt the remaining 2 tablespoons of butter and combine with the rest of the cheese, the thyme, and the poppy seeds. Spread the dough in the pan, and pour the cheese mixture over the top.
7. Bake 20 to 25 minutes, cut into squares, and serve hot.

16 SQUARES

In the language of herbs and flowers,
thyme represents courage.

Dill Cornbread with Sausage

Hot sausage adds a little spice to this cornbread, which would be an unusual item on a brunch buffet or even a main dish at supper. Of course the sausage could be sweet instead; in fact, the bread can be made without any sausage at all. If you like dill, try doubling it.

2 tablespoons butter
3 medium onions, thinly sliced
½ pound hot Italian sausage
2 cups unbleached all-purpose
   flour
1 cup yellow cornmeal
¼ cup sugar

½ teaspoon baking soda
2 eggs
¼ cup vegetable oil
1¾ cup plain low-fat yogurt
¼ cup snipped dill
Salt and freshly ground pepper

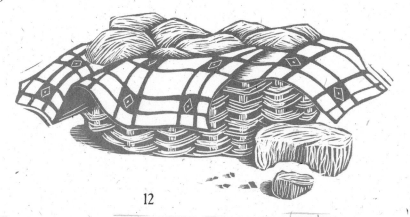

Onion Chowder with Sage

Say "chowder" and you think of clam, corn, or fish chowder. Each usually has onions as an ingredient. So why not go for the onions and forget the rest?

3 tablespoons butter	1½ quarts boiling water
2 cups chopped yellow onions	1 teaspoon salt
1 garlic clove, minced	Freshly ground pepper
2 tablespoons minced fresh sage	1 quart milk, warmed
1¼ pounds potatoes, peeled and	2 teaspoons minced fresh thyme
diced (4 cups)	2 tablespoons chopped fresh parsley

1. In a large soup pot, melt the butter and cook the onions slowly until they are golden. For the last 5 minutes, add the garlic and sage. (If you want to make this soup without fat, substitute chicken broth for the butter.)
2. Add the potatoes and the boiling water. Reduce heat and simmer for 25 minutes, or until the potatoes are tender. Add the salt, pepper to taste, milk, and thyme.
3. Reheat but do not boil. Serve the chowder in preheated bowls, and garnish with the parsley.

3½ QUARTS

16

1. Preheat the oven to 400°F, and grease a 10-inch round baking dish, at least 1½ inches deep.
2. Melt the butter in a medium-size skillet, and sauté the onions until they are soft and golden.
3. Remove the casings from the sausage. Slice the sausage about ¼-inch thick, and bake in a shallow pan for 15 minutes. Drain off the fat, turn the oven down to 350°F, and spread the sausage in the baking dish.
4. Combine the flour, cornmeal, sugar, and baking soda in a large bowl.
5. In a small bowl, beat 1 egg and combine with the oil, 1 cup of the yogurt, and the dill. Blend into the dry ingredients until everything is just mixed. Pour over the sausage slices.
6. Spread the onions on top of the batter. Combine the rest of the yogurt, the other egg, and a dash of salt and pepper, and pour over the onion layer.
7. Bake for 25 to 30 minutes, or until a toothpick inserted near the center comes out clean.

20 PIECES

13

Chinese Green-Onion Pancakes

Whether it's a crepe, a tortilla, or a pancake, every country seems to have its blintz — a delicate little flour product that can be enhanced with all sorts of fillings and can appear as the prologue, the main drama, or the curtain call. These traditional Chinese pancakes are made with the simplest of ingredients, and they are a treasure on the table, either as a first course or, if you make enough, as a lunch entree with salad. Cake flour ensures tenderness, so it's worth the effort to get it.

2 cups cake flour	4 tablespoons unbleached
1 teaspoon salt	all-purpose flour
1 cup plus 2 tablespoons	1 bunch scallions (6 or 7)
peanut oil	¼ cup sesame oil
1 cup boiling water	2 tablespoons minced fresh parsley

1. Combine the flour and salt, stir in 2 tablespoons of the peanut oil, and add the boiling water, mixing until a ball of dough starts to form.
2. If the dough is sticky, work in as much of the all-purpose flour as is necessary to make it smooth. Knead for 4 or 5 minutes, adding flour as needed to get a smooth, elastic dough. Cover with plastic wrap. Set aside for 20 minutes.
3. In the meantime, clean and mince the green and white parts of the scallions, removing the roots and at least 1 inch from the tops. You should have ½ cup.

14

4. On a lightly floured surface, make a long, ropelike roll out of the dough, about 1 inch in diameter. Divide it into 16 parts.
5. Keeping the other pieces covered with plastic wrap, take one piece of the roll and, using a rolling pin, form a 5-inch circle. Brush with sesame oil, sprinkle with some of the scallions and a pinch of parsley, and roll it up, pinching the ends to seal.
6. Coil the roll into a circle, pinch the end to secure it, and set it aside on a floured platter. Repeat this process with the other 15 pieces, and let them stand for about 30 minutes.
7. Then roll out the coils again, this time into 4-inch circles, and leave for another 30 minutes. The pancakes can be stacked with wax paper between them.
8. Preheat the oven to warm. Heat a heavy skillet, and when it is hot, add the remaining cup of peanut oil. Fry the pancakes until they are golden brown and a little crispy on both sides. Remove with a slotted spatula and place on paper towels to drain some of the oil.
9. As they are cooked, the pancakes can be transferred to a cookie sheet in the warm oven.

16 PANCAKES

15

1. Preheat the oven to 400°F, and grease a 10-inch round baking dish, at least 1½ inches deep.
2. Melt the butter in a medium-size skillet, and sauté the onions until they are soft and golden.
3. Remove the casings from the sausage. Slice the sausage about ¼-inch thick, and bake in a shallow pan for 15 minutes. Drain off the fat, turn the oven down to 350°F, and spread the sausage in the baking dish.
4. Combine the flour, cornmeal, sugar, and baking soda in a large bowl.
5. In a small bowl, beat 1 egg and combine with the oil, 1 cup of the yogurt, and the dill. Blend into the dry ingredients until everything is just mixed. Pour over the sausage slices.
6. Spread the onions on top of the batter. Combine the rest of the yogurt, the other egg, and a dash of salt and pepper, and pour over the onion layer.
7. Bake for 25 to 30 minutes, or until a toothpick inserted near the center comes out clean.

20 PIECES

Chinese Green-Onion Pancakes

Whether it's a crepe, a tortilla, or a pancake, every country seems to have its blintz — a delicate little flour product that can be enhanced with all sorts of fillings and can appear as the prologue, the main drama, or the curtain call. These traditional Chinese pancakes are made with the simplest of ingredients, and they are a treasure on the table, either as a first course or, if you make enough, as a lunch entree with salad. Cake flour ensures tenderness, so it's worth the effort to get it.

2 cups cake flour	4 tablespoons unbleached
1 teaspoon salt	all-purpose flour
1 cup plus 2 tablespoons	1 bunch scallions (6 or 7)
peanut oil	¼ cup sesame oil
1 cup boiling water	2 tablespoons minced fresh parsley

1. Combine the flour and salt, stir in 2 tablespoons of the peanut oil, and add the boiling water, mixing until a ball of dough starts to form.
2. If the dough is sticky, work in as much of the all-purpose flour as is necessary to make it smooth. Knead for 4 or 5 minutes, adding flour as needed to get a smooth, elastic dough. Cover with plastic wrap. Set aside for 20 minutes.
3. In the meantime, clean and mince the green and white parts of the scallions, removing the roots and at least 1 inch from the tops. You should have ½ cup.

4. On a lightly floured surface, make a long, ropelike roll out of the dough, about 1 inch in diameter. Divide it into 16 parts.
5. Keeping the other pieces covered with plastic wrap, take one piece of the roll and, using a rolling pin, form a 5-inch circle. Brush with sesame oil, sprinkle with some of the scallions and a pinch of parsley, and roll it up, pinching the ends to seal.
6. Coil the roll into a circle, pinch the end to secure it, and set it aside on a floured platter. Repeat this process with the other 15 pieces, and let them stand for about 30 minutes.
7. Then roll out the coils again, this time into 4-inch circles, and leave for another 30 minutes. The pancakes can be stacked with wax paper between them.
8. Preheat the oven to warm. Heat a heavy skillet, and when it is hot, add the remaining cup of peanut oil. Fry the pancakes until they are golden brown and a little crispy on both sides. Remove with a slotted spatula and place on paper towels to drain some of the oil.
9. As they are cooked, the pancakes can be transferred to a cookie sheet in the warm oven.

16 PANCAKES

Onion Chowder with Sage

Say "chowder" and you think of clam, corn, or fish chowder. Each usually has onions as an ingredient. So why not go for the onions and forget the rest?

3 tablespoons butter
2 cups chopped yellow onions
1 garlic clove, minced
2 tablespoons minced fresh sage
1¼ pounds potatoes, peeled and
    diced (4 cups)

1½ quarts boiling water
1 teaspoon salt
Freshly ground pepper
1 quart milk, warmed
2 teaspoons minced fresh thyme
2 tablespoons chopped fresh parsley

1. In a large soup pot, melt the butter and cook the onions slowly until they are golden. For the last 5 minutes, add the garlic and sage. (If you want to make this soup without fat, substitute chicken broth for the butter.)
2. Add the potatoes and the boiling water. Reduce heat and simmer for 25 minutes, or until the potatoes are tender. Add the salt, pepper to taste, milk, and thyme.
3. Reheat but do not boil. Serve the chowder in preheated bowls, and garnish with the parsley.

3½ QUARTS

Highly esteemed as a healing herb, sage derives its name from the Latin salvia, *"to heal."*

Vichyssoise with Parsley

In the winter, call it leek and potato soup and serve it with chunks of the vegetables, hot as can be to dispel the cold of January or February. In summer, puree it smooth as silk, chill it, and present it in frosty glass soup plates, with a sprig of parsley and a chip of red pepper on top, to battle the heat of an August day.

> 2 tablespoons butter
> 2 cups leeks, sliced into 1-inch pieces
> 2 tablespoons minced fresh Italian flat-leaf parsley
>   plus 6 whole sprigs
> 1½ pounds potatoes, peeled and diced (5 cups)
> 4 cups chicken broth
> 1 cup light cream or low-fat milk
> ⅛ teaspoon white pepper
> Salt
> ½ sweet red pepper, cut in six pieces

1. Melt the butter in a large soup pot, and sauté the leeks about 4 minutes, or until they are as limp as a well-cooked noodle. After the first minute or so, add the minced parsley.
2. Add the potatoes and the chicken broth. Bring to a boil, then reduce the heat to low and simmer for 15 to 20 minutes, or until the potatoes are tender.

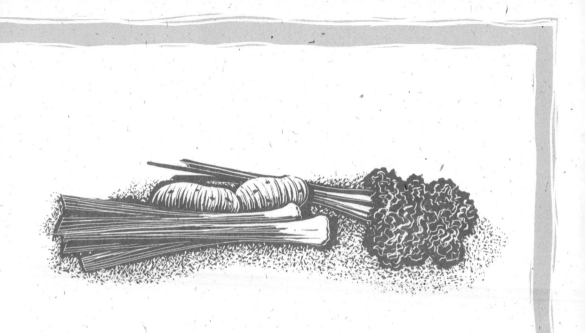

3. If you want to serve the soup hot, stir in the cream or milk, the pepper, and salt to taste. Reheat without bringing to a boil.

4. If you want a formal or chilled soup, let it cool a little and then puree in a blender. Stir in the cream or milk and the pepper. Season to taste with the salt. Chill well and garnish with parsley sprigs and a piece of red pepper.

6 SERVINGS

French Onion Soup

The French make any number of onion soups, but on American menus the name has come to mean a certain hearty blend of onions, beef broth, and flavorings, topped with a crust of bread and some kind of cheese. Here's one way to do it, using thyme.

>   *4 tablespoons butter*
>   *5 cups of yellow onions, peeled and thinly sliced*
>   *2 garlic cloves, chopped*
>   *3 teaspoons minced fresh thyme*
>   *8 cups beef broth*
>   *Salt and freshly ground pepper*
>   *Olive oil*
>   *6 slices of French bread (baguette)*
>   *8 ounces Gruyère cheese, shredded (2 cups)*

1. Melt the butter in a soup pot, and add the onions. Cook the onions over low heat for 15 to 20 minutes, turning them frequently. They should be golden but not browned. Add the garlic and thyme and cook another 3 minutes.
2. Add the beef broth, bring to a boil, and then reduce to a simmer for 20 minutes. Taste and add salt and pepper if needed, remembering that the broth, butter, and cheese all have salt.

3. While the soup is cooking, brush oil on both sides of the French bread slices. Place in the oven at 325°F and bake for about 10 minutes.
4. Preheat the broiler. Using individual ovenproof soup bowls, place a slice of bread in each and put a teaspoonful of cheese on the bread. Fill the bowls with hot soup and cover with the rest of the cheese.
5. Place the bowls under the broiler for about five minutes, or until the cheese is bubbling. Serve immediately.

6 SERVINGS

Marshoushy

Bulgur, a tasty, cracked wheat, is a staple in the Middle East and has become well known to health-food devotees and tabbouleh lovers in this country. This Lebanese salad, brought home by my traveling sister, takes a slightly different tack. Like tabbouleh, however, it's minty.

> ½ cup bulgur
> ½ cup boiling water
> ½ cup olive oil
> 6 yellow onions, chopped (2 cups)
> ½ jalapeño pepper, seeded and finely chopped
> 1 medium cabbage, finely chopped
> 1 can (8 ounces) tomato sauce
> 2 tablespoons finely chopped mint
> Salt
> Spinach or lettuce leaves
> Sprigs of fresh mint for garnish

1. In a small bowl, soak the bulgur in the boiling water. Set aside for about 20 minutes until softened and then drain if any liquid remains.
2. Heat the oil in a medium skillet, and sauté the onions until they are light brown. Stir in the chopped jalapeño.

3. Add the cabbage and cook over low heat for 5 to 10 minutes, stirring occasionally. The cabbage should be a little crisp rather than soft.
4. Stir in the bulgur. Add the tomato sauce, mint, and salt to taste. Simmer 20 minutes, stirring occasionally.
5. Refrigerate for about 2 hours. Serve in a mound on spinach or lettuce leaves, garnished with sprigs of mint.

6 SERVINGS

Green Onions and Oregano with Garbanzo Beans

Garbanzo beans, also known as chickpeas, come dried or canned. If you decide to use dried beans, cover them in water, soak overnight, drain, and then cook them for an hour, or until tender. Otherwise, use the canned beans, which are also excellent — especially with fresh oregano and parsley.

3 cups garbanzo beans, cooked
Juice of 2 lemons
4 tablespoons olive oil
Salt and freshly ground pepper
4 green onions, sliced in thin rings
2 teaspoons minced fresh oregano
2 tablespoons chopped fresh parsley
Frilly lettuce leaves

1. Heat the garbanzo beans to a boil, drain, and place in a salad bowl.
2. Combine the lemon juice, oil, salt and pepper to taste, onions, and oregano in a jar with a tightly fitting lid, and shake well. Pour over the warm beans and toss gently to avoid crushing the beans.
3. Sprinkle the parsley over the top, cover with plastic wrap, and chill. Serve on a bed of frilly lettuce.

SERVES 4

Oregano is said to calm upset stomachs, headaches, and other complaints of the nerves.

Dilled Scallion Salad

For part of the summer, you can get scallions or green onions by thinning the onions in the garden. But by the time the cucumbers come along, the onions are too big for that. So you need to plant Japanese bunching onions, which grow lovely stalks but not large bulbs.

6 scallions
2 medium young cucumbers
¼ cup snipped dill
4 tablespoons white wine vinegar
1 tablespoon sugar
Freshly ground black pepper

1. Remove the roots and the top ½ inch or so of the scallions. Then slice them lengthwise into quarters. Cut the shredded lengths into 1-inch pieces.
2. Peel and slice the cucumbers paper thin.
3. Place a layer of cucumbers in a shallow bowl, top with a layer of onions, and sprinkle with dill. Continue layering until the vegetables are all used.
4. Combine the vinegar and sugar, stirring or shaking until the sugar is dissolved. Pour the dressing over the vegetables, cover with plastic wrap, and chill for about 1 hour.

4 SERVINGS

During the Middle Ages, drinking wine with a bit of dill was believed to enhance passion.

South-of-the-Border Salad

On a hot summer day, a glass bowl full of well-chilled vegetables and herbs, including tender scallions from the garden, will be the perfect accompaniment for grilled chicken or fish. If cilantro is not your favorite herb, substitute parsley.

2 cucumbers, shredded (4 cups)
3 well-ripened tomatoes, chopped (2 cups)
¾ cup minced scallions, white and green parts
¼ cup minced sweet green pepper
¼ cup minced sweet red pepper
Juice of 2 limes (⅓ cup)
¼ cup extra virgin olive oil
2 tablespoons minced fresh cilantro
Salt and freshly ground black pepper
½ jalapeño pepper, seeded and minced

1. Place the cucumbers, tomatoes, scallions, and peppers in a large glass bowl. Whisk the lime juice and oil together with the cilantro, salt and pepper to taste, and jalapeño.
2. Pour the dressing over the vegetables, and toss gently until all are coated. Chill.

6 TO 8 SERVINGS

Cilantro seeds — or coriander — were found in the tombs of pharaohs.

Pissaladière Niçoise

If it's *Niçoise*, it has olives, garlic, olive oil, tomatoes, basil, anchovies — some or all. They are ingredients that relish living together: Their aroma tantalizes the nostrils during cooking, their colors please the eye, their taste fulfills expectations. Pizza is not the most elegant way to sample *Niçoise*, but it's a good one.

1 package dry yeast	2 garlic cloves, chopped
1¼ cups lukewarm water	15 black olives or Greek olives, pitted
3 cups unbleached all-purpose flour	1 large ripe tomato
1 teaspoon salt	6 anchovies
1 tablespoon sugar	1 tablespoon minced fresh basil
6 tablespoons olive oil	½ cup grated and mixed Parmesan
6 large Spanish onions, sliced	and Romano cheeses
(about 4 cups)	

1. Dissolve the yeast in ¼ cup of the lukewarm water and let stand for 3 or 4 minutes.
2. Sift 2½ cups of the flour, the salt, and the sugar into a bowl. Stir in the rest of the water and add the yeast mixture.
3. Add 2 tablespoons of the olive oil and knead for 2 or 3 minutes. Add more flour to make the dough easy to handle. Knead until smooth.
4. Place the dough in an oiled bowl, cover with a towel, and let rise for about 45 minutes.
5. While the dough is rising, heat the remaining 4 tablespoons of olive oil in a large skillet, add the onions, and cook over low heat slowly for 30 to 40 minutes. They should be soft and translucent, not brown, so temperature is crucial. Add the garlic for the last 10 minutes. Remove from heat and let cool.
6. Preheat the oven to 400°F. Chop the olives. Cut the tomato crosswise and scoop out most of the seeds, then chop it.
7. Roll out or form the dough into a 12-inch circle in a slightly oiled pizza pan. Layer on the cooked onions, arrange the olives and anchovies in a star pattern on top of the onions, and scatter the chopped tomato and the basil over the top. Sprinkle with the grated cheeses.
8. Bake for about 15 minutes, or until the edges of the dough have browned slightly and the cheese has melted.

6–8 PIECES

Pasta with Garlic and Herb Sauce

Red sauce is what most people eat on pasta. But pasta takes to so many kinds of sauces that it's a good idea to branch out now and then. This sauce, chock-full of herbs, makes a great vegetarian main dish and can be served over linguini, fusilli, or one of the short, curly noodles, like rotini, that hold a sauce so well.

> 1 stick butter
> ¼ cup chopped garlic (about 24 medium cloves)
> 2 tablespoons finely chopped fresh basil
> ½ teaspoon finely chopped fresh rosemary
> ½ teaspoon finely chopped fresh thyme
>   White pepper
> 2 cups half-and-half or light cream
> 1½ pounds pasta
>   Salt
> ¼ cup minced fresh Italian flat-leaf parsley

1. Start a large pot of water boiling for the pasta. In the meantime, melt the butter in a large skillet and gently sauté the garlic for 2 minutes. Add the basil, rosemary, thyme, pepper to taste, and half-and-half or cream.

2. Simmer slowly for approximately 5 minutes, until the cream is reduced and the sauce has thickened. Drop the pasta into the boiling water and cook according to package directions.
3. Salt the sauce to taste and stir in the parsley.
4. Drain the pasta, place in a warmed pasta bowl, pour the sauce over the top, and mix lightly.

6 SERVINGS

Thyme and Onion Pie

The Chinese have a gift for taking a small amount of meat — chicken, pork, or beef — and surrounding it with vegetables and rice or noodles in such a way that you have the illusion of considerably more. This onion pie, inexpensive and fragrant with thyme, does much the same thing. It can be made with a prepared pie shell, a flaky pastry of your own, or this baking-powder biscuit crust.

CRUST INGREDIENTS
- 1 cup flour
- 1½ teaspoons baking powder
- ½ teaspoon salt
- 2 tablespoons butter
- ½ cup low-fat milk

FILLING INGREDIENTS
- 3 tablespoons butter
- 4 large yellow onions, chopped (2 cups)
- 1 tablespoon minced fresh thyme
- 3 eggs
- ¼ teaspoon ground cloves
- ½ teaspoon salt
- Freshly ground black pepper
- 1 cup low-fat yogurt
- 3 slices Canadian bacon or thinly sliced ham

1. Preheat the oven to 350°F. Sift the flour and combine with baking powder, salt, butter, and milk for the baking-powder biscuit crust. Roll out the dough to a ¼-inch thickness, and line the bottom of a 9-inch pie pan, leaving extra around the edge.
2. Double the extra dough over and crimp into a fluted rim around the pan. Bake the crust for 5 minutes, remove from the oven, and increase the oven temperature to 400°F.
3. While the crust is baking, make the filling. Melt the butter in a large skillet, and sauté the onions with the minced thyme until the onions are soft but not browned. Remove from heat.
4. In a small bowl, whisk the eggs. Add the eggs, cloves, salt, and pepper to taste to the onions and toss gently. Then add the yogurt. Pour the mixture into the pie pan.
5. Cut the Canadian bacon or ham into small squares and arrange decoratively over the top of the onion mixture. Bake about 15 minutes, or until the meat is crisp and the crust is light brown. Cut into wedges and serve immediately.

4–6 SERVINGS

Savory Quiche with Onions

Perhaps real men don't eat quiche, or perhaps they've never tried it. In any case, they should like this one. It's not the least bit wimpy, what with a high onion content and the bite of cayenne.

PASTRY DOUGH FOR QUICHE

1⅓ cups unbleached all-purpose flour
½ cup very cold butter, cut into inch-long pieces
¼ cup ice water
Olive oil

QUICHE INGREDIENTS

3 tablespoons extra virgin olive oil
2 tablespoons butter
1½ pounds white onions, peeled and sliced
1 cup half-and-half
½ teaspoon cayenne pepper
2 teaspoons minced fresh savory
Salt
4 eggs
¼ cup minced fresh parsley

1. To make the pastry dough, place the flour and butter in a food processor and process for no more than 10 seconds. The mixture will have the consistency of meal. Slowly pour the ice water through the feed tube while the processor is running. Stop when the dough forms a ball. Remove and shape into a flat round.
2. On a lightly floured board, roll out the pastry until it is large enough for a 10-inch quiche or pie pan. Brush a thin layer of the oil on the pan and roll out the pastry slightly larger than the pan. Crimp the edges.
3. Preheat the oven to 350°F. Heat the oil and the butter in a large skillet, add the onions, and cook over low heat for at least 30 minutes. The onions will be soft and nearly translucent — but not browned.
4. In a bowl, combine the half-and-half with the cayenne, savory, and salt to taste. Add the eggs and beat until foamy. Stir in the parsley.
5. Spread the onions over the pastry in an even layer. Pour in the egg mixture, making sure it trickles down through the layer of onion. Bake for 30 to 35 minutes, or until firm and browned on top.
6. Cut in wedges and serve warm.

8–10 SERVINGS

Deviled Shrimp and Onion Salad

Rich, roasted peppers, black olives, yellow lemon, and red onion put a riot of color around pink shrimp in this summer salad. Serve it in a cut glass or black bowl for a spectacular effect.

2 pounds fresh shrimp
1 lemon, thinly sliced
1 red onion, thinly sliced
½ cup chopped black Greek olives
2 tablespoons chopped roasted
    sweet green peppers
1 bay leaf
Juice of 1 large lemon
    (about ½ cup)

¼ cup extra virgin olive oil
1 tablespoon white wine vinegar
2 garlic cloves, put through a press
1 tablespoon dry mustard
¼ teaspoon cayenne
Salt and freshly ground pepper
½ cup coarsely chopped fresh parsley

1. Shell and devein the shrimp. Cook for 3 minutes in lightly salted boiling water.
2. Drain the shrimp and place in a large salad bowl to cool. Add the lemon, onion, olives, and roasted peppers. Toss.
3. Crush the bay leaf very fine with a mortar and pestle or in a blender. Combine in a small bowl with the lemon juice, olive oil, vinegar, garlic, dry mustard, and cayenne. Mix thoroughly, and add salt and pepper to taste.

4. Pour the dressing over the shrimp and toss gently, taking care not to break the shrimp.
5. Sprinkle the parsley over the top, cover tightly with plastic wrap, and refrigerate for at least 2 hours.

4 SERVINGS

Sole with Chives and Leeks

Here's a dish that embraces three members of the allium family: leeks, chives, and shallots. Beat and heat gently to make sure the sauce doesn't curdle; then add fresh chopped parsley at the last minute for a bright contrast with the pale green of the leeks and the white fish.

6 tablespoons butter
6 medium leeks, sliced
¼ cup snipped fresh chives
2 shallots, peeled and chopped (2 tablespoons)
¼ cup dry white wine
¾ cup half-and-half
4 egg yolks
¼ teaspoon white pepper
2 teaspoons lemon juice
Salt
6 sole or flounder fillets
¼ cup chopped fresh parsley

1. Preheat the oven to 325°F.
2. Melt 2 tablespoons of the butter in a heavy skillet, and sauté the leeks 3 to 5 minutes, or until they are limp. Transfer to a bowl and set aside.
3. Melt the rest of the butter and sauté the chives and shallots for 2 minutes. Add the wine and half-and-half, and simmer for about 1 minute.
4. In a small bowl, beat the egg yolks and add about a tablespoon of the sauce to them. Then add the yolks to the rest of the sauce.
5. Heat gently. Add the white pepper, lemon juice, and salt to taste, and heat until the sauce thickens slightly. Mix about a quarter of the sauce with the leeks.
6. Spoon the leek mixture onto each sole fillet; then roll up the fillets. Place the rolls seam-side down in a baking dish, pour the remaining sauce over the fish, and cover with aluminum foil.
7. Bake for 30 minutes, uncover, sprinkle the parsley over the top, and serve.

6 SERVINGS

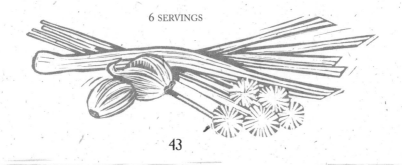

Chive and Dill Sauce for Fish

One of the great things about chives is that you can plant a little bunch almost anywhere among your perennials and they'll be there, ready to use. If you live in the snowy north, their green shoots are a reassuring sign of spring. A member of the onion family, chives work well both for mild onion flavor and as a garnish. Use the feathery leaves of dill in this sauce, and garnish each plate with a handsome head of dill in bloom.

> 4 tablespoons sweet butter
> 2 tablespoons snipped fresh chives
> 1 teaspoon lemon juice
> ½ teaspoon dry mustard
> 2 teaspoons finely snipped fresh dill
> 4 fish fillets

1. Melt the butter in a medium-size skillet, add the chives, and cook for about 2 minutes over low heat.
2. Blend in the lemon juice, dry mustard, and dill.
3. Bake, broil, or poach the fish fillets. Pour the sauce over the fillets and serve.

4 SERVINGS

Onions, Mushrooms, and Tarragon

As a sauce for sole or a relish on the side, this combination of onions, hot peppers, shiitakes, and tarragon adds zip.

2 large white onions, thinly sliced
2 teaspoons salt
1½ tablespoons extra virgin olive oil
6 large shiitake caps, sliced
1 habanero or other hot chile pepper, finely chopped
1 tablespoon chopped fresh parsley
½ cup white wine vinegar
2 tablespoons chopped fresh tarragon
1 cup plain lowfat yogurt

1. Place the onions in a glass bowl, sprinkle with the salt, cover with cold water, and let stand for 15 to 20 minutes.
2. Heat the oil in a skillet and sauté the shiitake slices over low heat for 5 minutes. Add the pepper and parsley. Cook another 5 minutes. Set aside.
3. Drain the onions. Combine the vinegar and tarragon and pour over the onions. Let the mixture stand for about 5 minutes.
4. Combine the onions with the mushrooms, pepper, and herb mixture. Stir in the yogurt. Serve chilled or at room temperature.

2 CUPS

Elissa's Jambalaya

Once upon a time, there was a recipe. Then Tim got his hands on it and tinkered with it. He passed it on to Ann, who changed it some more. She gave it to Elissa, who decided on the turkey sausage. When it came to us, we jiggled it a little, too. Try it, then change it again if you like.

2–3 tablespoons extra virgin olive oil	¼ cup minced fresh parsley
5 large onions, chopped	2 tablespoons hot sauce
2 sweet green peppers, chopped	¼ cup soy sauce
4 ribs of celery, chopped	3 tablespoons minced fresh thyme
4 garlic cloves, chopped	Freshly ground black pepper
1 can (28 ounces) crushed tomatoes	1½ pounds shrimp, shelled and deveined
2 cans (16 ounces) chicken broth	1½ pounds bay scallops
1 package (6 to 8) turkey sausages	2 cups cooked rice
½ cup diced ham	

1. Heat the oil in a Dutch oven or soup pot. Add the onions and sauté for 2 or 3 minutes. Then add the green peppers, celery, and garlic. Continue to cook until the vegetables begin to soften.
2. Add the crushed tomatoes and the chicken broth. Cover and simmer for 30 minutes.

3. In the meantime, place the turkey sausages in a shallow pan and bake in the oven for 15 minutes, or until they are browned. When they are cool enough to handle, cut them into ¾-inch slices.
4. Add the ham, parsley, hot sauce, soy sauce, thyme, and black pepper to taste to the onion-tomato mixture. Cover and simmer another 20 minutes.
5. Add the sausage, shrimp, scallops, and rice to the pot. Cover and simmer a final 25 minutes.

SERVES 10–12

Onion Rice with Tarragon

It's a little hard to tell whether this is an onion dish with rice or a rice dish with onions — but it's easy to tell that it's delicious. There are, however, a lot of onions to peel, so the cook may be sobbing before all is done. (See the introduction for ways to avoid the tears.)

> 2 tablespoons unsalted butter
> 6 large onions, sliced
> 2 teaspoons minced fresh tarragon
> 4 quarts of water with ½ teaspoon salt
> 2 cups uncooked brown rice
> Salt and freshly ground pepper
> ½ cup white wine or water
> ¼ cup half-and-half
> 4 ounces Gruyère cheese, grated (1 cup)

1. Preheat the oven to 300°F.
2. Melt the butter in a large ovenproof skillet or casserole dish. Add the onions and tarragon, and cook over low heat until they are buttery and soft.
3. In a large saucepan, bring the salted water to a boil, add the rice, and boil for 5–10 minutes to soften. Drain the rice and add it to the onions, along

with salt and pepper to taste. Cover and bake for 50 to 60 minutes. (The onions will provide enough liquid for the rice to cook.)

4. When done, cool the casserole slightly, and then refrigerate. Up to this point, the recipe may be prepared the day before.

5. To serve, add the white wine or water and reheat over low heat. In the meantime, mix the half-and-half with the cheese and heat gently. When the rice is hot, combine the rice and cheese mixtures.

10 SERVINGS

Walter's Herbed Chicken with Onions

It's hard to get a recipe from Walter because he's the kind of cook who surveys the refrigerator and cupboards, gets out a pot, and starts putting various things in it. (His friends can testify that the method works for him just about every time.) He has tried here to provide real quantities for ingredients and says this should cook until it's like stew, with the onions turning to juice and becoming almost unrecognizable.

6 medium yellow onions   6 medium-size ripe tomatoes
3 garlic cloves   3 boneless, skinless chicken
1 tablespoon minced fresh oregano   breasts, halved
¼ cup light soy sauce   1 tablespoon minced fresh basil

1. Peel and thinly slice the onions. Crush the garlic. Place them in a 2- or 3-quart casserole with the oregano. Add the soy sauce.
2. Preheat the oven to 325°F.
3. Wash and slice the tomatoes about ½-inch thick. Arrange the chicken breasts in a single layer atop the onions, and cover them with a single layer of sliced tomatoes. Sprinkle the basil over the top, and cover the casserole.
4. Bake in the oven for 2 hours. (It can bake up to 3 hours if guests are late.) If the dish seems to be cooking too fast, turn the oven down to 300°F.

6 SERVINGS

Veal Scallopini with Onions

Start this with really good veal, and ask the butcher to pound it thin. If it's not really thin, put the slices between pieces of wax paper and pound it some more. With its butter, oil, herbs, onions, and white wine, this is a superb dinner party dish.

1½ pounds veal scallopini,
    pounded thin
4 tablespoons flour
Salt and freshly ground black pepper
2 tablespoons extra virgin olive oil
3 tablespoons butter

2 yellow onions, peeled and sliced
2 tablespoons chopped fresh
    oregano
2 tablespoons chopped fresh parsley
½ cup dry white wine

1. Dredge the scallopini in the flour, adding salt and pepper to taste, shaking to remove excess flour. Heat the oil in a large skillet and quickly brown the veal on both sides, removing the pieces to a warm plate as they are done. Each slice will take only a minute or so per side.
2. Pour any excess oil out of the pan, but do not rinse the pan. Melt the butter and sauté the onions until they are tender. Add the oregano and parsley, and return the veal to the pan, turning the slices to coat them with onions and butter. Add the wine and simmer until everything is hot.

4 SERVINGS

Beef, Beer, and Bay Leaves

On a cold winter weekend, get this stew going in the morning and let it simmer its way to full flavor. Once made, you can refrigerate it, skim off any fat that appears on the surface, and reheat it for dinner.

¼ cup unbleached all-purpose flour
¼ teaspoon salt
¼ teaspoon freshly ground black pepper
2 pounds lean beef, trimmed of fat and cut into cubes
12 small onions, peeled
1 bottle (12-ounces) dark beer
2 cups beef broth
2 cups water
2 tablespoons red wine vinegar
1 tablespoon brown sugar
2 garlic cloves, chopped
2 tablespoons chopped fresh marjoram
2 bay leaves

1. In a plastic bag, mix the flour, salt, and pepper. Add the beef cubes and toss until they are coated with the mixture. Shake off the excess flour.

2. In a Dutch oven or soup pot, combine the beef cubes, half the onions, the beer, the beef broth, and the water. Bring to a boil and skim off any foam that appears. Add the vinegar, brown sugar, garlic, marjoram, and bay leaves.

3. Bring to a boil again, reduce the heat, and simmer for about 1½ hours. Add the rest of the onions. Simmer for another 30 to 45 minutes, or until the beef is really tender. Remove the bay leaves if they are still whole.

SERVES 4

*Bay is symbolic
of peace and victory.*

Sherried Onions with Dill

This version of creamed onions carries a hint of sherry and a touch of fresh dill.

Main ingredients
2 pounds small white onions
1 tablespoon finely snipped dill
¼ cup medium-dry sherry

White sauce ingredients
4 tablespoons butter
4 tablespoons unbleached all-purpose flour
2 cups low-fat milk at room temperature

1. Peel the onions and boil them until they're just cooked but not falling apart. Drain them and place in a baking dish.
2. Preheat the oven to 325°F.
3. To prepare white sauce in microwave, cook the butter and flour for 2 minutes, stirring after the first minute. Add the milk and cook 4 minutes more, stirring after 2 minutes. If the sauce has not thickened, cook for another 2 minutes.
4. Blend the dill and the sherry into the white sauce and pour over the onions. Bake for 15 or 20 minutes.

6 SERVINGS

Savory Onions with a Glaze

With this unique dish, once you've peeled all the onions, the work is done.
The other ingredients are simple to prepare, and then the oven takes over.
The result is an almost caramelized sweetness, with a hint of cayenne.

> 36 small white onions
> ⅔ stick butter
> 1 beef bouillon cube
> 1 tablespoon brown sugar
> ½ teaspoon salt
> ⅛ teaspoon cayenne
>   Dash of nutmeg
>   Dash of ground ginger
> 2 teaspoons minced fresh savory

1. Fill a large pot with water and bring to a boil. Drop in the onions and
   let cook for a minute. Drain and peel the onions. Preheat oven to 350°F.
2. Melt the butter in a casserole dish in the oven. Remove, and stir in the
   bouillon cube, brown sugar, salt, cayenne, nutmeg, ginger, and savory.
3. Add the onions and toss gently until they are well coated. Cover and
   bake for about 1 hour, occasionally checking to make sure the onions are
   not sticking to the casserole dish

6–8 SERVINGS

New-Fashioned Boiled Onions

Boiled onions, slathered with butter, salt, and pepper, were always part of our traditional Thanksgiving dinner. But they had to cook a long time, and so they'd start to separate. Delicious as the rounded layers were, you'd wish for a whole one. Here's how to keep the taste, add some new flavor, and hold the onions together using the microwave.

> 10 medium yellow onions, peeled
> 1 tablespoon water
> 2 tablespoons butter
> 2 teaspoons minced fresh chervil

1. Place the peeled, whole onions in a microwavable casserole dish with the water and butter. Cover tightly and microwave on high for 7 to 8 minutes.
2. Sprinkle the chervil over the top and serve.

4 SERVINGS

Grilled Onions with Herbs

Our friend Sel, who has tried grilling practically everything, recommends putting a piece of slate or some other fireproof slab on the grill, then placing foil packages of vegetables on the slate. You won't have to watch in dismay while nicely cooked onions slip into the fire. (Sel suggests roasting garlic, another member of the onion family, in foil on slate, too.)

8 large white or yellow onions
1 stick butter, melted
¼ cup chopped fresh parsley
1 tablespoon chopped fresh sage

1 garlic clove, minced
2 tablespoons grated Parmesan and Romano cheeses, mixed

1. Peel the onions, slice about ¼ inch off the top, and hollow out the center, leaving plenty of wall. Chop what you remove.
2. In a saucepan, melt the butter and sauté the chopped onion for about a minute. Remove from heat and add the parsley, sage, garlic, and grated cheeses. Scoop the mixture into the hollowed onions.
3. Place the filled onions on heavy-duty aluminum foil and wrap them tightly. Put them on the grill for at least 30 minutes — and beware of escaping steam when you open the package.

8 SERVINGS

Braised Leeks with Dill

Leeks are kind of a sleeper. You don't see them on restaurant menus very often, except in soup, and you don't eat them at home very often, either. But they're sweet, oniony, and versatile. Here they team with tomatoes, onions, and dill. (Their one disadvantage is they're hard to clean. Unless a recipe says otherwise, slit them lengthwise and flush them with water until the grit is gone.)

8 medium leeks
2 tablespoons butter
2 tablespoons extra virgin olive oil
2 medium onions, peeled and sliced into rings
2 large ripe tomatoes, peeled and chopped
½ cup chicken broth
½ cup dry white wine
Salt and freshly ground black pepper
1 tablespoon snipped fresh dill

1. Trim the leeks, removing the coarse upper leaves and cutting off all but 2½ inches of the green leafy part. Wash thoroughly. Drain and cut each leek into 1½- to 2-inch pieces.
2. In a large skillet, melt the butter, add the oil, and sauté the onions slowly, until they are golden and translucent but not fried. Add the leeks and the tomatoes.
3. Add the chicken broth, white wine, and salt and pepper to taste. Bring to a boil, reduce the heat, and simmer gently until the leeks are tender but not mushy.
4. Transfer to a heated serving dish. Garnish with the dill and serve.

6 SERVINGS

Scalloped Onions with Savory

For no apparent reason, thin slices of veal are called scallops. In addition, when you bake a sliced vegetable — like potatoes — in milk or cream, it's called scalloped, or even escalloped. This has nothing to do with the seashell or its little edible nuggets. But scalloped is good, and it works with onions.

6 medium yellow onions
5 tablespoons butter
4 tablespoons flour
1 cup light cream or low-fat milk, at room temperature
1 cup low-fat cottage cheese

2 teaspoons minced fresh savory
2 tablespoons chopped fresh parsley
Salt and white pepper
3 scallions, sliced in ¼-inch rings
1 cup finely crushed crackers

1. Slice the onions as thin as possible and cook in boiling water until soft. Drain.
2. Melt 4 tablespoons of the butter, mix in the flour, and gradually add the cream or milk, stirring until thick. Add the cottage cheese, savory, parsley, and salt and white pepper to taste.
3. Preheat the oven to 350°F. Arrange a layer of onions in a buttered 1½-quart casserole, cover with a layer of the cheese mixture, and continue layering until both are used up. Scatter the scallions over the top. Cover with the crackers, and dot with the remaining butter.
4. Bake for about 20 minutes.

4 SERVINGS

Onions Provençale

When you're pulling the onions right out of the garden, and they're filled with moisture and sweetness, remember how good zucchini Provençale is in the midst of summer. This recipe echoes the goodness of that one and adds basil, the herb of Provence.

4 tablespoons extra virgin olive oil
6 large onions, sliced in rings
2 garlic cloves, chopped
Salt and freshly ground black pepper

2 tablespoons minced fresh basil
1 large ripe tomato
12 black olives, pitted
½ teaspoon lemon zest

1. In a large skillet, heat the oil and add the onions, separating most of the rings. Cook gently for about 15 minutes; then add the garlic, salt and pepper to taste, and the basil. Cover and cook for another 5 minutes.

2. Cut the tomato into eighths and add to the onion mixture. Stir in the olives and lemon zest. Simmer for another 10 minutes.

4 SERVINGS

Index

Converting Recipe Measurements to Metric

Use the following formulas for converting U.S. measurements to metric. Since the conversions are not exact, it's important to convert the measurements for all of the ingredients to maintain the same proportions as the original recipe.

When The Measurement Given Is	Multiply It By	To Convert To
teaspoons	4.93	milliliters
tablespoons	14.79	milliliters
fluid ounces	29.57	milliliters
cups (liquid)	236.59	milliliters
cups (liquid)	.236	liters
cups (dry)	275.31	milliliters
cups (dry)	.275	liters
pints (liquid)	473.18	milliliters
pints (liquid)	.473	liters
pints (dry)	550.61	milliliters
pints (dry)	.551	liters
quarts (liquid)	946.36	milliliters
quarts (liquid)	.946	liters
quarts (dry)	1101.22	milliliters
quarts (dry)	1.101	liters
gallons	3.785	liters
ounces	28.35	grams
pounds	.454	kilograms
inches	2.54	centimeters
degrees Fahrenheit	$5/_9$ (temperature − 32)	degrees Celsius

While standard metric measurements for dry ingredients are given as units of mass, U.S. measurements are given as units of volume. Therefore, the conversions listed above for dry ingredients are given in the metric equivalent of volume.